Exploring tough questions facing youth today

DO THE RIGHT THING
Ethics Shaped by Faith

ISBN 978-1-949628-09-8
Printed in the United States of America.
10 9 8 7 6 5 4 3 2 1   22 21 20 19

Published by The Pastoral Center, http://pastoral.center.

Developed in partnership with MennoMedia and Brethren Press. Series editors: Fumiaki Tosu, Ann Naffziger, and Paul Canavese. *Do the Right Thing*: Writer, Jennifer Halteman Schrock. Project editor, Lani Wright. Staff editors, Susan E. Janzen, Julie Garber, and James Deaton. Updated design, Paul Stocksdale.

All rights reserved. Purchase of this book includes a license to reproduce this resource for use in a single parish, school, or other similar organization. You are allowed to share and make unlimited copies only for use within the organization that licensed it. If you serve more than one organization, each should purchase its own license. You may not post this document to any web site without explicit permission to do so. Outside of these conditions, no part of this book may be reproduced in any form or by any means, electronic or mechanical, including photocopying, recording, taping, or via any retrieval system, without the written permission of The Pastoral Center, 1212 Versailles Ave., Alameda, CA 94501. Thank you for cooperating with our honor system regarding our licenses.

For questions or to order additional copies or licenses, please call 1-844-727-8672 or visit http://pastoral.center.

Portions of this work © 2019 by The Pastoral Center / PastoralCenter.com. Adapted and published with permission from Generation Why Bible Studies. © 1995, 2014 Brethren Press, Elgin, IL 60120 and MennoMedia, Harrisonburg, VA 22803, U.S.A. All rights reserved.

Unless otherwise noted, the Scripture passages contained herein are from the *New Revised Standard Version of the Bible*, copyright © 1989 by the National Council of the Churches of Christ in the United States of America. Used by permission. All rights reserved.

Bible-based Explorations of Issues Facing Youth

>> OVERVIEW

When conversing online, the acronym IRL stands for "in real life." The virtual world of social media, text chats, blogs, and more have the power to remove us from the real world. What we experience online can skew our perspective on what it means to be human. It can numb us, incite us, distract us, depress us, confuse us, and make us rude or impatient. Strangely, this supposedly "social" and "connected" technology can profoundly disconnect us from others.

Religious faith can also place us in a bubble, especially when it distances us from others. When we keep the prophetic message at a safe distance, obscured in theological language and abstractions, we are missing the whole point. And when we see our parish as an insider club that serves itself, we can forget the radically inclusive message entrusted to us: God's love is for *everyone*, and God expects us to transform the *whole world* through that love.

Through the incarnation, God showed up in the real world to show us that our faith is not just about talking the talk, but also walking the walk. It can be risky. It can be confusing. It can hurt. But living out our faith can also bring us great purpose, peace, and joy.

This series connects the Bible with the tough questions that youth (and adults) encounter in their neighborhood, in school, among friends, and even online. This process will help you as a leader break open these issues in a fun and meaningful way, sparking conversation and the kind of life change Jesus invites us to embrace.

>> THE ROLE OF PARENTS

As children enter middle school and high school, they become more independent, self-reliant, and, well, self-centered. This can bring parents to make assumptions that this is the time to step back, giving their child more space to form their identity. While there is truth to that at some level (adolescents definitely shouldn't be smothered), this is a stage of life when parents should in fact *lean in*. The apparent confidence and bluster youth show on the outside can mask the insecurity and confusion on the inside. Youth need their parents to be involved more than ever.

>> WHOLE FAMILY FORMATION

Parents are the primary teachers of their own children, and parishes are waking up to the fact that faith formation programs need to bring parents into the process if they hope to see faith passed on to the next generation. Recent studies give us more and more evidence that the role of parents is the most important factor in determining whether a child will embrace faith as they move toward adulthood. Research from the Center for the Applied Research on the Apostolate shows that parents who talk about their faith and show through their actions that their faith is important to them are more likely to have children who remain Catholic.

More about Whole Family Formation >>>>

To learn more about how your parish can take a comprehensive whole family approach to faith formation, visit **GrowingUpCatholic.com**.

While whole family events with elementary-aged children are on the rise, the role of parents can be an afterthought in youth ministry. We have designed the sessions in this series to work with or without parents present, and we encourage you to offer them as parent-child events.

If you choose to involve parents, it is important to consider before each session how to best do so. Many of the activities in this series are high-energy, creative, or silly. Some parents may need some encouragement to get out of their heads and have fun with the group. A few activities involving physical contact would be inappropriate for parents and youth to participate together, and we have noted them as such.

There are a number of ways to approach discussions with parent participation. Unless you have a small group, you will likely want to break into smaller groups for conversation. Some youth may be self-conscious and unable to be completely honest and open in a group situation with a parent present. For this reason, you may choose in some cases to assign parents to different groups from their own children, or to have separate parent and child groups altogether. Be sure to cover expectations around confidentiality. It is inappropriate for a parent (or youth) to share with another parent what their child said in a small group.

Note that even if parents and their children do not share all conversations together in the session, they will still have a valuable shared experience and can have extended conversations about it later.

>> THANK YOU

The role you play in gathering, animating, praying with, and forming youth is a valuable one. Thank you for all you do to serve the church and its families!

Bible-based Explorations of Issues Facing Youth

DO THE RIGHT THING
Ethics Shaped by Faith

>> INTRODUCTION

This unit on right and wrong is rooted in a phrase from the past. Our grandparents heard it from their parents, and they passed it on to our parents. "Remember who you are..." they said when someone asked for the car keys or went on a date. "Remember who you are" was shorthand for everything the community stood for and the family had attempted to instill.

This unit is less a workshop in decision-making skills than it is a course in Christian identity. It proceeds on the assumption that if we are clear about who we are, what to do next will become a little clearer. People of faith have not always agreed about what's right and what's wrong, but they *have* managed to agree on what's real: a Creator who is worth worshiping; a Christ whose humiliating death was turned to loving power by the resurrection; the Spirit of God at work in our world today; a place called church where we express and experience the community of Christ; and the freedom to be forgiven and start over when we mess up.

This unit pairs everyday youth issues with convictions basic to the biblical story. "How might Jesus' teachings and life example make a difference in what we do about violence?" it asks. "How might the activity of the Holy Spirit in our lives make a difference in the way we respond to authority figures?"

Youth who complete this unit can have a clearer sense of what it means to claim a Christian identity. This foundation can serve them well as they sort out the gritty details of what's right and what's wrong.

>> ADVANCE PREPARATION

1. *Set up a "Decision Clinic" or "Clearness Committee"*

Most youth find it hard to talk about the situations they are really dealing with, and not all groups trust each other. Consider providing another setting where more personal sharing can take place. Find a time when you and another adult can be available for individuals or small groups who want to talk about really difficult personal decisions or experiences. In Quaker circles, this is called a clearness committee, and is requested when someone seeks to reach clarity on how to respond to a concern or dilemma. A key rule for clearness committees is that committee members are forbidden to speak to the focus person in any way except to ask honest, open questions. No advice should be given.

»»» EXTENDER SESSION

The extender session suggests special activities related to the issue of the unit. Extender sessions help accommodate the diversity of parish schedules. Since each unit is undated, youth may study units in their entirety and still participate in special events of the parish that get scheduled simultaneously with youth group time. Extender sessions can be used anytime, but the one for this unit best follows **Session 6**. Calculate now whether or not you will be using the extender session.

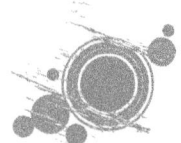

2. Watch for adults with a story to tell

Youth learn how to make good choices mainly through watching mature adults grapple with right and wrong. Who has a story to tell about his or her own youth? What sticky ethical situations have come up in your parish in the past five years? Is there someone willing to talk to the youth about what happened and how the church handled it? The **extender session** asks you to find several adults who can join you for a panel discussion.

THE TEACHING PLAN: The parts of the session guide

» **Faith identity.** An overarching Christian affirmation appropriate to the issue of the session.

» **Faith story.** The session is rooted in this Bible passage.

» **Faith focus.** The story of the passage in a nutshell.

» **Session goal.** The entire session is built around this goal. What changes—in knowledge, attitude, and/or action—do you desire in your group?

» **Materials needed and advance preparation.** This is what you will need if the session is to go smoothly. You'll feel more at ease if you've taken care of these details before you meet your group.

»» FROM LIFE TO BIBLE TO LIFE

The teaching plan is called *life-centered*. However, when we write each session, we always begin with scripture. We ask, what does this particular passage say, especially to youth? Each session moves from life to Bible to life. So the Bible is really at the center of this way of teaching.

In every session we try to hit upon a tough question that youth might ask. Find out what questions on this issue are important for your group. Feel free to bring your own input and invite your group members to add their own experiences.

»» TEACHING THE SESSION

The five step-by-step movements will carry you from *life to the Bible and back to life*. Each session takes about 45 to 50 minutes. If there is a handout sheet for the session, take note of any complementary activities and stories.

1. **Focus.** Intended to create a friendly climate within the group and to *draw attention* to the issue.

2. **Connect.** Invites participants to *express* their own life experience about the issue, through talking, drawing, role playing, and other activities. Also uses memory, reason, or imagination to get the group thinking about *why* they view the issue the way they do.

3. **Explore the Bible.** What does the Bible *say* about the issue? With a minimum of lecturing, dig into the faith story and search for answers to questions raised in the first activities. The Insights from Scripture section will help clarify the faith story. Help participants discover how the faith community understands the Bible passage.

4. **Apply** the faith story. What does the Bible passage *mean* for contemporary life? This is the "aha!" moment when participants realize the faith story has wisdom for *their* lives.

5. **Respond.** Why does the Bible passage *matter*? What will the group do about the issue in light of what they have learned from their own experiences set alongside the faith story? How can we *live* the faith story rather than pass it off as a mere intellectual exercise?

6 In Real Life | Do the Right Thing

❯❯ LOOK AHEAD

Here are reminders for what you need to do for the next session or two.

❯❯ INSIGHTS FROM SCRIPTURE

Here is a resource for Explore the Bible. Don't try to use all the material given. Take what you need to lead the session and answer questions your group may have. Let the Insights section inspire you to think and study more about the passage for the session.

❯❯ HANDOUT SHEETS

Occasionally, there will be a handout sheet to complement your session. If you choose to use this, make enough copies for the group in advance of the session. These sheets may include questions, stories, agree/disagree exercises, charts, pictures, and other materials to stimulate thinking and discussion.

Generally, no participant preparation is required unless the session plan calls for you to contact selected group members for specific tasks.

Acknowledgment: A particularly helpful resource is *The Church as Parable: Whatever Happened to Ethics?* by David Schroeder and Harry Huebner.

>>> SESSION 1

CREATOR WORTH WORSHIPING >>>

>> FAITH IDENTITY
We are heirs to the story of a loving Creator worth worshiping.

>> KEY VERSES
"I am the Lord your God, who brought you out of the land of Egypt, out of the house of slavery; you shall have no other gods before me." (Exodus 20:2-3)

>> FAITH STORY
Exodus 32:1-8; Exodus 20:1-21

>> FAITH FOCUS
While Moses encountered God on Mount Sinai and received the ten commandments, the Israelites grew impatient. They asked Aaron to make them gods and ended up worshiping a golden calf. The two incidents contrast two understandings of God: one phony and one worth bowing down to.

>> SESSION GOAL
Help participants recognize the relationship between how we envision God and what we consider right and wrong.

>> **Materials needed and advance preparation**

- Several high school yearbooks or photo albums (College yearbooks might work better for an older group)
- Chalkboard/chalk or newsprint/marker
- Bibles
- Copies of the handout sheet for Session 1
- Empty boxes about the size of a cereal box (*Option A* in Apply)
- Large sheets of white paper
- Drawing materials
- Magazines that can be cut, scissors (*Option A* in Apply)
- Glue or tape
- Idol-building materials (see *Option D* in Apply)
- Song books (*Option* in Respond)

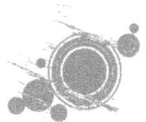 # TEACHING PLAN

1. FOCUS 5 minutes

Bring several old photo albums or high school yearbooks to the meeting and leave them out where participants can browse through them as they gather. Write the phrase,

Remember who you are

on newsprint or a chalkboard. Begin the session by asking the group what they think this phrase means. Then ask, *What does it have to do with deciding the right thing to do?*

2. CONNECT 5 minutes

Continue by drawing attention to the yearbooks you brought in. Ask:

- *Why do schools create yearbooks? Why is it so interesting to look at them and remember?*
- *What can you tell about a school by studying its yearbook? Do different schools have different identities? How is that identity passed from one class to the next? Can you tell who goes to what school just by how they act?*
- *Where do we get our sense of right and wrong?*

The main point to get across is that what we do flows out of who we understand ourselves to be and who we look up to.

3. EXPLORE THE BIBLE 10 minutes

Shift to this activity: Hold up a Bible. Then say, *This is a yearbook of sorts, filled with snapshots that tell us who we are and who God is. Like a yearbook, it tells stories that remind us of where we came from and whose we are. Today we're going to look at two snapshots from Exodus: one that shows us a god who is phony and one that shows us a God worth worshiping.*

Ask your group what pictures come to mind when they think of the book of Exodus. Make sure they are clear that this session's Bible passage comes from the giving of the law on Mount Sinai following the Hebrews' dramatic escape from Egypt across the Red Sea. Even youth who have very little church background may be familiar with the Exodus story from movies like *Prince of Egypt*.

Give two good readers copies of the handout sheet. They should stand on opposite sides of the room to read it so that it is clear they are telling two different stories. This reading contrasts the "I AM" God with a handmade image of a god, but ask your group what *they* heard and how the two snapshots of God were different. List responses on a chalkboard or newsprint. Important to include:

- The golden calf is handmade; the God on the mountain is beyond human control.
- The golden calf is made visible by an image; the God on the mountain is made visible by a way of life.

Also ask: *What kinds of idols do people worship today? Can people believe in God and still be worshiping an idol?*

>> **Option:** For a more in-depth study, have participants turn to Exodus 20 and 32:1-8 and re-read these passages themselves. For additional discussion, try these statements out on your group. Ask:

Which ones would most people believe today? Which statements are opposites?

- God has told us what is good.
- Right and wrong is pretty much left up to us.
- Right worship is important for right behavior.
- Who we worship in church on Sunday doesn't affect how we make decisions about right and wrong the rest of the week.
- People no longer have problems with idolatry today.
- Any false center to our lives or false understanding of God is an idol.

>> **HOW ARE FAITH MEMORIES CREATED?**

- headline experiences
- repetitive experiences
- personally touching events
- significant relationships

4. APPLY 20 minutes

>> **Option A:** Divide participants into teams of two or three. Have each group design an "idol" that shows a false god people build their lives around today. Each team needs a box to use as a base for their idol, enough paper to cover the box, and access to markers, magazine photos, etc. While teams work, ask them to think about this question: *If this idol is "god" (money, beauty, etc.), what kinds of behavior might we expect to see?*

Allow 10-15 minutes work time, then bring the teams back together and have each group present its idol and the behavior the idol suggests. Examples: If a national flag is god, it would be wrong to allow another country to oppose it. If money is god, one should always seek jobs that make the most money possible. If God is always an angry judge, then one can never make a mistake or tolerate mistakes in others.

An idol is made visible by an image; the God on the mountain is made visible by a way of life.

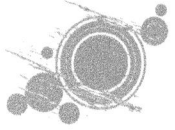

>> **Option B (time-saver option):** If your group is small and your time limited, have each person draw an idol rather than organizing teams and building with boxes. Somewhere on the drawing they should:

- name the idol
- list kinds of behaviors that would be expected for that idol

Or bring in your own examples of idols (see examples above) and discuss what kind of behavior they would call forth.

>> **Option C (extra challenge option):** Rummage through your local thrift store for cheap costume jewelry and have your group make their idols out of earrings and knick-knacks as the Israelites did. Can they come up with something worth bowing down to?

>> **Option D (for camp/retreat setting):** Divide participants into teams of two or three. Have each group design an "idol" that shows a false god people build their lives around today. Build "idols" out of cloth dipped in plaster of Paris:

- 1½ parts plaster of Paris
- 1 teaspoon powdered alum for each cup water
- 1 part water

Mix plaster of Paris and alum, add water, and stir until smooth.

Dip cloth (gauze, old sheeting, even paper towels will do) into plaster mixture, and drape over a bottle, cardboard, or other frame. Groups will have 15-20 minutes to shape the cloth before it dries very hard.

While teams work, ask them to think about this question: *If this idol is "god"* (money, beauty, etc.), *what kinds of behavior might we expect to see?* (Examples are listed under **Option A** above.)

5. RESPOND 5 minutes

Put your idols in the trash or recycling. If participants have worked hard on their creations this might not be so easy! But idols need to be done away with.

Ask participants to think of life situations that have caused them to struggle with right and wrong. If you have time, share briefly; if not, challenge your group to think about this question over the next few days: *How might different gods or understandings of God lead to different actions in these situations?*

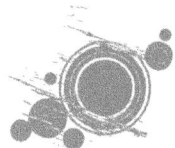

LOOK AHEAD

Skim the rest of the sessions in this unit. It will help you know where you are going and get tuned in to the approach this unit takes. Also read the Bible passages for each session. It is easier to teach a passage if it has been rattling around in your head for several weeks.

When you close, hold up a Bible and one of the yearbooks or photo albums you brought. Remind participants that this, too, is a book that helps us remember who we are, because it tells stories that remind us of who we are created to be and who we might become. It gives us pictures of a God worth building a life around and shows us what it was like for people a lot like us to honor this Creator. Why do we need to know this? Because, slowly but surely, we become like the One we worship. And who we worship determines how we act.

Suggested benediction: *Remember who you are—you are heirs to the story of a loving Creator worth worshiping.*

>> **Option:** If your group is willing to sing together, close with a familiar song.

 # INSIGHTS FROM SCRIPTURE

Many youth today (and adults too) find it hard to believe that God is real. The existence of God may be just something they teach you in Sunday school when you're a kid. In the secular world where we spend most of our time, it can be embarrassing or unlawful to even mention God. For many North Americans, God is on par with Santa Claus and the tooth fairy.

Those of us who are believers struggle to affirm the reality of an unseen God and to make sure we are not seduced into false understandings of who that God is. The Bible passage for this session presents us with an ancient version of this same struggle.

>> ## TO SEE GOD

The Israelites, camped out in an unfamiliar wilderness with their harrowing escape from Egypt still fresh in their experience, allowed insecurity to overwhelm them. It seemed Moses had disappeared. The mysterious 'I AM' God he told them about seemed remote and unreal. So they turned to Aaron and begged for a God they could see.

Why did the Israelites want to worship a golden calf? For one thing, it was a familiar god. Bull symbolism was used throughout the ancient Near East to represent deity. For another, it was a symbol of both fertility and valor in battle, sometimes associated with human war leaders as well as gods. No doubt the Israelites felt safer in hostile territory with the image of a warlord in their midst.

But as we see from God's reaction and Moses' destruction of the idol later in chapter 32, God did not wish to be associated with a phony golden calf made out of recycled earrings. Nor did God care for the wild partying that resulted from this kind of worship. The biblical tradition insists that this kind of god is not real, even if visible; nor does its worship lead to the good life.

>> WHAT KIND OF GOD, THEN?

We believe in a Creator who made the world and named the good. The Bible describes God as the maker of heaven and earth. Usually we think of this as the physical world: sea, sky, plants, etc. We remember the creation story where God proclaimed each day's work good. But, perhaps even more important, is the idea that *God is the maker of the moral order.* God "has told you, O mortal, what is good," the prophet Micah says in Micah 6:8. "And what does the Lord require of you but to do justice, and to love kindness, and to walk humbly with your God?"

Exodus 20 is one of the places where God names what is good. We may be inclined to think of the ten commandments as a list of restrictive rules, but what they really are is a vision of the good life. Certain behaviors simply do not work well for human beings. They destroy human community and alienate us from the Creator. The book of Exodus—and in fact all of the Bible—could be called God's "I Have a Dream" speech. It tells the truth about human brokenness and sin, but also shows us who God created us to be and who we might become.

We believe in a God who is revealed primarily through a way of life. If we could step back in time and visit an ancient Near Eastern temple at the time of the Exodus, we would find an image or idol of this people's god. It would be located in the holiest spot in the center of the temple. If, on the same trip, we could visit the Hebrew tabernacle described in Exodus, and were permitted to peek into its holiest spot, we would find something different. There would be no image of God because the Israelites did not believe it was possible to capture God this way. Instead, we would find a set of stone tablets with a vision of the good life carved on them. What God has chosen to reveal to us is not the divine face but the divine dream for creation: a way of life that leads to wholeness and peace.

We believe in a God who created us in the divine image. We are not permitted to *make* images of God, but we are called to *be* God's image: for that is what we were created to be (Genesis 1:27-28). We are intended to embody God's love and care for each other and for all the earth. Slowly but surely, we become like the One we worship. And who we worship determines how we act.

> **What God has chosen to reveal to us is not the divine face but the divine dream for creation: a way of life that leads to wholeness and peace.**

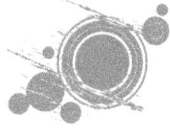

Story in Stereo

Exodus 19:3-6; 20:1-17; 32:1-8

In Real Life
Exploring tough questions facing youth today

> **An idol is made visible by an image; the God on the mountain is made visible by a way of life.**

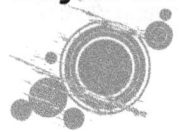

Voice 1: Moses went up to Mount Sinai. God called to him from the mountain and said, "This is what you are to say to the people of Israel: You have seen what I did to Egypt when they enslaved you, and how I carried you on eagles' wings and brought you to myself. Now if you obey me fully and keep my covenant, then out of all nations you will be my treasured possession. Although the whole earth is mine, you will be a special holy nation."

Voice 2: When the people saw that Moses was so long in coming down from the mountain, they gathered around Aaron and said, "Come, make us gods who will go before us. As for this fellow Moses who brought us up out of the land of Egypt, we don't know what has happened to him."

Voice 1: I am the Lord your God, who brought you out of Egypt, out of the land of slavery. You shall have no other gods before me.

Voice 2: Aaron answered them, "Take off the gold earrings that your wives, your sons, and your daughters are wearing, and bring them to me." So all the people took off their earrings and brought them to Aaron.

Voice 1: You shall not make for yourself an idol…. You shall not bow down to idols or worship them…. You shall not misuse the name of the Lord….

Voice 2: Aaron took what they handed him and molded it into an idol in the shape of a calf. Then they all said, "These are our gods who brought us out of the land of Egypt."

Voice 1: Remember the sabbath day by keeping it holy…. Honor your father and your mother so that you may live long in the land the Lord your God is giving you.

Voice 2: When Aaron saw this, he built an altar in front of the calf and announced, "Tomorrow there will be a festival to the Lord." So the next day the people got up early and brought offerings and sacrifices to the calf.

Voice 1: You shall not murder, you shall not commit adultery, you shall not steal, you shall not give false testimony against your neighbor, you shall not covet.

Voice 2: Afterward they sat down to eat and drink and got up to party.

Voice 1: Then the Lord said to Moses, "Go down, because your people, whom you brought up out of Egypt, have become corrupt. They have been quick to turn away from what I commanded them and have made themselves an idol cast in the shape of a calf."

Permission is granted to photocopy this handout for use with this session.

>>> SESSION 2

THE SWORD IN THE GARDEN >>>

>>> FAITH IDENTITY
We are followers of a Christ who died rather than harm others.

>>> KEY VERSE
When those who were around [Jesus] saw what was coming, they asked, "Lord, should we strike with the sword?" (Luke 22:49)

>>> FAITH STORY
Luke 22:47-53

>>> FAITH FOCUS
Jesus was arrested by an armed crowd while praying on the Mount of Olives. His disciples asked whether they should defend him. When one zealous follower cut off the ear of a servant, Jesus healed the man and said, "No more of this!" He was then seized and crucified.

>>> SESSION GOAL
Help participants embrace Jesus' death and resurrection as a costly rejection of violence and a revelation of the way God overcomes evil.

>>> Materials needed and advance preparation
* An assortment of "weapons" (see Focus)
* Copies of the handout sheet for Session 2
* Bibles
* Study Luke 22–24
* Two pair of large shoes or sandals (*Option B* in Apply)
* Research various year-long volunteer service programs for students to consider in their future (*Option C* in Apply)
* Large sheets of white paper; markers and pens (*Option B* in Respond)

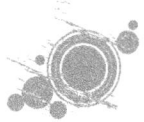

TEACHING PLAN

1. FOCUS 3 minutes
Pass around a box containing a variety of items that could be used as weapons (baseball bats, bricks, bottles, surgical instruments, etc.). You could also use photos or toy representations of guns, bombs, or tanks. Have each person choose one to hold throughout the session.

Instead of having a box of "weapons," you could also ask each person to draw a picture of a weapon and a situation in which it would be tempting to use it.

2. CONNECT 10 minutes

Ask each person to think of a situation when it would be tempting to use their object to harm another person.

Some of the weapons or photos you brought might suggest a street fight or self-defense; others might suggest war or oppression. The broader variety of weapons you have, the greater number of situations they will call to mind. Allow a minute or two of thinking time, then ask for volunteers to share their scenarios. Ask: *What is at stake here? Why would violence be tempting?*

3. EXPLORE THE BIBLE 7 minutes

Shift to this activity by saying: *You may be surprised to see weapons in church. We sometimes forget Jesus lived in the real world and had to make choices about weapons and violence, too.*

Most of us have heard the crucifixion story so often we might lose sight of how or why it happened the way it did. But we might have a better understanding of why Jesus died and what his death means for our lives if we can imagine a different sequence of events.

Read aloud the fictional account of Jesus' arrest on the handout sheet. You may find it interesting to approach this "text" with all seriousness and see how far you get. The object is to shock them into hearing the real story with new ears. Once participants have realized your version of the story is not from the Bible, distribute copies of the handout sheet and let them see "A Story that Never Happened" and the genuine text from Luke 22:47-53 side by side.

>> **Option:** For a more in-depth study, use Bibles instead of a handout, or move from the handout to Bibles. It is helpful to see this story in the context of surrounding passages. Note, for example, that the passage immediately before Luke 22:47-53 describes an intense prayer session. What is the relationship between prayer and the ability to trust God in the face of violence, as Jesus did? The following passage, meanwhile, offers an interesting commentary on human nature. The disciple who was so brazen with a sword in his hand was later unable to admit he knew Jesus.

4. APPLY 15 minutes

>> **Option A:** Move from the Bible story to some of the violent possibilities your participants talked about during the Connect section. Questions to ask:

How might

    a) *the way Jesus lived, and*

    b) *the way he died, and*

    c) *the fact that he rose from the dead*

affect the way Christians make decisions about using violence?

Although the resurrection is not in view in this Bible passage, it is a crucial part of the story. It is Jesus' resurrection that vindicates the life he lived and the death he died. Make sure you get there at some point.

What about _____ (sticky situations your group described)? Why are we obligated to reject violence as Jesus did? Isn't he a special case?

>> **Option B:** This passage can be linked with youth experience rather easily, especially if you have read the complete Passion story (Luke 22–24) and can fill in a few details. Remember that there are two places to stand in this story: Jesus' shoes and the disciples' shoes. Although we might like to model ourselves on Jesus' self-assurance in the face of a violent situation, most of us are closer to the disciples' dilemma.

Bring out the two pair of shoes or sandals and ask participants to take turns standing in each of them. Say: *Imagine yourself in the garden of Gethsemane the night Jesus was arrested. What do you see or feel when you stand in Jesus' shoes? In Peter's shoes?*

Below are some clues.

Youth experiences Jesus would understand:

- Being lonely: Neither Jesus' friends nor his enemies understand what he's about.
- Being ridiculed: Jesus is repeatedly made fun of for not saving himself. See Luke 23:35-39.
- Being treated unfairly: Jesus is an innocent guy arrested while praying, of all things.

Youth experiences the disciples would understand:

- Being embarrassed or reprimanded by your parents or a teacher
- Watching someone you care about look foolish and weak
- Being confused about what was expected of you
- Being angry at an adult or respected leader for letting you down
- Being afraid you'll get into **BIG** trouble

>> **Option C:** Find out where people in your group are with respect to exposure to various volunteer service programs (a year or more) that are open to young adults and/or college graduates. Are they are aware these are options for post high school and college? Even if they haven't considered exploring this as an option, they may have friends or relatives who have served in organizations like the Peace Corps, the Jesuit Volunteer Corp, Americorps, etc. There may also be young adults from your parish who have been a member of such an organization. You may consider inviting them in to speak to the youth.

Research a few programs and lay out some of the possibilities as well as the similarities and differences. For example, the Peace Corps entails oversees work and is not faith based. The Jesuit Volunteer Corps is primarily for young people who want to serve in the US although there are some communities abroad. JVC is a Catholic program. The Americorps strives to "strengthen communities and develops leaders through direct, team-based national and community service." Like the Peace Corps it is not faith based.

Some students may need/want paid opportunities which are available in some programs (like Americorps.) Others cover basic living expenses and student loan deferment.

>>>
The Jesuit Volunteer Corps engages brave young leaders in life-changing service, living and working with those in need to build a more just and hopeful world.

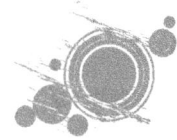

5. RESPOND 10 minutes

Direct attention back to the weapons. You can do this either by simply saying: *Look at your weapons again*, **OR** by incorporating **Option A** or **Option B**, below, which involve a little more action. Whichever you choose, close with the prayer time described below.

Invite participants to return to the situations they described earlier in the Connect section; they are to pray for the healing of the enemy they envisioned harming. Acknowledge this challenge by saying something like: *I'm asking you to try something really difficult.* Any sane person faced with a violent situation feels more inclined toward retaliation than prayer—yet prayer was an important preparation to Jesus' choice in the garden of Gethsemane.

Allow a period of silence. Then close with the following prayer:

> Merciful and loving God,
> > we ask you with all our hearts to bountifully pour out on our enemies whatever will be for their good.
> Above all, give them a sound and uncorrupt mind with which they might honor and love you and also love us.
> Do not let their hating us turn to their harm.
> Lord, we ask that they be changed, and that we be changed.
> Do not separate them from us by punishing them;
> > deal gently with them and join them to us.
> Help us to see that we have all been called to be citizens of the everlasting city;
> > let us begin to love each other now because love is the end we seek. AMEN
> > > (adapted from a 16th-century English prayer, author unknown)

》》 **Option A:** Have a mock wrestling session. Take your group to a space where they have room to move and ask participants to imagine they are in a wrestling match with the weapons they are holding; then find a pose that can be held for a while. Pray for healing while holding the wrestling pose.

》》 **Option B:** Give each person sheets of paper and have them trace the weapon they are holding. Collect the weapons and have everyone write a prayer for the healing of an enemy inside the outlined space.

Suggested benediction: *Remember who you are—you are followers of a Christ who died rather than harm others.*

LOOK AHEAD

Next session includes an option which asks you to come up with a current video clip. You will have an easier time finding one if you informally poll youth on their favorite shows or movies.

Jesus died knowing the awful consequences if his peace plan was rejected. Still, he did not rely on the sword to keep it safe.

INSIGHTS FROM SCRIPTURE

Some Christians are content to say that Jesus died for our sins and leave it at that. Others, however, find it important to understand *how* he died. Jesus died preaching a peace plan. He opened his ministry with an announcement of good news to the poor, healing to the sick, freedom for prisoners, and God's favor to a land that was overrun and overlooked.

Throughout the next several years, in an intensely charged political climate, Jesus lived out this vision and taught others how they might live justly and mercifully in spite of Roman oppression. He ate with tax collectors and invited them to reimburse their overburdened clientele. He ate with wealthy Pharisees and urged them to have lunch with people who couldn't invite them in return.

THE "WRONG" MESSIAH

Meanwhile, Jesus defied the traditional Jewish definitions of what it meant to be the Messiah and what the reign of God would look like. He did not organize an army. He did not drive the heathen out of Jerusalem. He did not defeat Rome. Instead, he healed Gentiles and told flattering stories about hated Samaritans. He offered both personal healing and a way of life that would heal society as a whole. Jesus died leaving the vision of the good life he preached in the hands of God.

It is important that we understand what was at stake that fateful night Jesus was arrested. The unjust death of a good man is a tragedy, but Jesus was the man who had proclaimed that the Spirit of the Lord was upon him. This was the man who had opened the eyes of the blind, outfoxed the Pharisees, and made demons tremble. When Jesus submitted to the cross, the vision of the life he preached seemed to die with him, leaving only destroyed hopes and despair.

THE WEEPING PROPHET

Jesus died weeping for Jerusalem. His recurring lament for the city that became his enemy and rejected the peace plan he preached is a frequently overlooked part of the Passion story. In Luke 19:41-44, when Jesus entered Jerusalem, he said, "If you, even you, had only recognized on this day the things that make for peace!" Twice in Luke 21 Jesus foretold the violence that would come upon Jerusalem. In Luke 23:28-30, on the way to the cross, he told weeping women not to weep for him but for themselves and their children.

Jesus' predictions came true some decades later when the Romans wiped out Jerusalem in the most destructive war of the ancient world. Jewish factions slaughtered one another while the Romans laid siege to the city and women and children starved. It seems that Jesus died knowing the awful consequences that would follow if his peace plan was rejected. Still he did not rely on the sword to keep it safe.

Jesus' death was a beginning, not an end. When we honor Jesus' death and resurrection, we celebrate the fact that God can bring life even out of utter failure and defeat. We proclaim that the reign of God cannot be defended by force, but neither is it crushed by death. We rejoice in God's way of doing battle with evil. Jesus' rejection of the sword in the garden does not give us all the answers to all the life-threatening situations we may be called upon to face. But it does orient us in a particular direction—nonviolence.

Christians affirm that Jesus of Nazareth is the best picture of God's character that we have. If this is so, then to accept Jesus as our Way to life means to let go of the weapons we would like to rely on for safety and put our trust in God instead.

> God can bring life even out of utter failure and defeat. We proclaim that the reign of God cannot be defended by force, but neither is it crushed by death.

A Story that NEVER Happened

In Real Life — Exploring tough questions facing youth today

> While Jesus was praying on the Mount of Olives with his disciples, suddenly a crowd came, and the one called Judas, one of the twelve, was leading them. He approached Jesus to kiss him, and thus betray him to his enemies. But Jesus drew back and cried to his disciples, "Now is the hour to strike back with the sword!" And they put to the sword the chief priests and the officers of the temple police and the elders who had rejected the coming of the Messiah. And all who had hoped to hand him over to the Romans to be killed were on that day destroyed, so that Jerusalem might be cleansed of its evil, for the kingdom of God was at hand.

... and a story THAT DID

> While [Jesus] was still speaking, suddenly a crowd came, and the one called Judas, one of the twelve, was leading them. He approached Jesus to kiss him; but Jesus said to him, "Judas, is it with a kiss that you are betraying the Son of Man?" When those who were around him saw what was coming, they asked, "Lord, should we strike with the sword?" Then one of them struck the slave of the high priest and cut off his right ear. But Jesus said, "No more of this!" And he touched his ear and healed him. Then Jesus said to the chief priests, the officers of the temple police, and the elders who had come for him, "Have you come out with swords and clubs as if I were a bandit? When I was with you day after day in the temple, you did not lay hands on me. But this is your hour, and the power of darkness!" (Luke 22:47-53)

Do the Right Thing : Session 2

Permission is granted to photocopy this handout for use with this session.

>>> **SESSION 3**

IN STEP WITH THE SPIRIT >>>

>> FAITH IDENTITY

We have been given the gift of the Holy Spirit as a touchstone for doing the right thing.

>> KEY VERSES

The fruit of the Spirit is love, joy, peace, patience, kindness, generosity, faithfulness, gentleness, and self-control. There is no law against such things. (Galatians 5:22-23)

>> FAITH STORY

Galatians 5:13-26

>> FAITH FOCUS

The Church in Galatia was struggling with whether or not they needed to keep the laws their Jewish ancestors passed down to them. Some congregations required Gentile converts to be circumcised. Paul explained the nature of spiritual freedom and tried to help the Galatians "live by the Spirit." While the presence of the Holy Spirit brings freedom from the spirit of the times, it also offers sound boundaries for behavior and for responding to other authority figures.

>> SESSION GOAL

As participants begin to separate from childhood authority figures and expand their search for other meaningful authorities, offer them the Holy Spirit as their guiding authority.

>> Materials needed and advance preparation

- Cooking utensils and ingredients as listed on the handout sheet for Session 3; kitchen (*Option A* in Focus)
- At least one copy of the handout sheet for Session 3
- Stack of magazines (*Option B* in Focus). Also, try this option yourself.
- Bibles
- Chalkboard/chalk or newsprint/marker
- Clips from current movies or TV sitcoms, media player (see *Option B* in Apply)
- Bowl of fruit

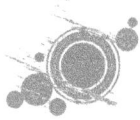

TEACHING PLAN

1. FOCUS 8-12 minutes

>> **Option A:** Place the cooking supplies and ingredients listed on the handout sheet in the middle of a table. Divide into two groups and announce that each group will get to bake a cake. Give the first group a copy of the handout sheet and tell them they must follow the recipe *to the letter*. If they alter the recipe in any way, you will dump out their cake batter. If you really want to frustrate this group, provide butter instead of margarine or the wrong shape pan.

In Real Life | Do the Right Thing   21

Tell the second group they are free to make the cake any way they like. Do not provide them with a recipe or allow them to consult the other group. Both groups may use the same ingredients.

The point of this exercise should soon become evident: Unnecessary rules are a problem and so is too much freedom. If your time is limited or you do not have access to an oven, it is not essential to complete the cake once this point is made. But if possible, your participants would probably enjoy eating cake at the end of the meeting and seeing how the "freedom cake" turned out.

>> **Option B:** Ask participants what comes to mind when they think of the word **freedom**. Provide a stack of magazines so they can find images that illustrate this word.

2. CONNECT 10 minutes

>> **Option A:** Discuss what happened during your Focus activity. If you used Focus, **Option A**, ask: *In your experience, is the life of faith more like baking a cake with too many senseless rules or like baking a cake without a recipe?* Try to hear from everyone.

If you used Focus, **Option B**, have each person show the magazine pictures they found. Ask: *Why did you choose these images to represent freedom?* Try to help participants analyze how our culture understands freedom. Do most of the people in their pictures look wealthy or prestigious? Ask what this has to do with freedom.

>> **Option B:** Ask participants to think of a time when they struggled with either too much or not enough freedom. It could be a time they found it hard to obey or respect an authority figure, or it could be a time they had more freedom than they knew what to do with.

Then, pair up and ask each pair to listen to each other's situations and then role-play them. Role-playing gives participants a chance to see how another person might respond to the problem situation or to try on the other side of the story. If you have plenty of time, ask one or two pairs to do their role-play for the whole group. Watching a role-play where a participants struggles with an unreasonable authority figure will add zing as you move into the Bible story.

The task of adolescence is to explore and challenge boundaries. For some youth, too much freedom may mean needing to find boundaries rather than challenge them.

3. EXPLORE THE BIBLE 6 minutes

Shift to this activity by saying: *Did you know that the Apostle Paul once told a group of people that they didn't* **have** *to obey authority figures? Can you believe he even got* **mad** *at them when they insisted on following rules?*

Give your group a brief background sketch on Paul's letter to the Galatians using the Insights from Scripture section. Explain why circumcision was an issue for this group of people.

Galatians 5:13-26 begins with the idea your participants have been working with: **freedom**. Read the first phrase of Galatians 5:13 and stop after "sisters." Ask participants to review in their minds what they learned about freedom so far in this session. Then ask them to read the rest of the passage with an eye for what Paul had in mind when he claims we are free. Write the questions in **Option A** of the Apply section on the chalkboard or newsprint while they are reading.

4. APPLY 10 minutes

>> **Option A:** Lead a discussion focused on two or three of the questions below. If your group tends toward silence, keep asking these questions and let them sit with them for a while. They require some thought. If your group is too active to reflect together for any length of time, **Option B** may work better. Or, keep this segment of the session brief and spend more time on Respond.

- *How is Paul's understanding of what it means to be free different from what our culture understands freedom to be?* (Comments in Insights about "freedom from"/"freedom for" may be helpful here.)
- *Have you ever experienced the presence of the Holy Spirit? How did you recognize it?*
- *How might claiming the Holy Spirit as your guiding authority make a difference in the way you respond to other authority figures?*
- *Is it always right to submit to authority figures? How and when should they be resisted?*

>> **Option B:** Show a short segment (1-3 minutes maximum) of a movie or current TV sitcom showing children interacting with parents or other authority figures in a cocky, disrespectful fashion. A clip from *Ferris Bueller's Day Off* or *Joan of Arcadia* would suffice. Show the clip one time without telling the group why they are watching it or what to look for. Then watch a second time and have them analyze the attitudes towards authority figures displayed in this scene. Focus on two or three of the questions below:

- *How do the characters respond to authority figures?*
- *What kind of internal authority guides the youth in this clip?* (The answer might be something like personal pleasure.)
- *Why does this kind of behavior attract viewers? Is it possible to write a screenplay scene that reflects the fruits of the Spirit and is still interesting?*
- *How does what you see in the media affect your relationships with authority figures?*
- *Paul paints a sharp contrast between life in the Spirit and what he calls the sinful nature. Is this still true today? How might people in step with the Holy Spirit seem odd or out of step with the society around them?*

5. RESPOND 5-7 minutes

If you did **Option B** under Connect: Bring out a bowl of fruit and give each person one piece. Have participants return to their original pairings and review the situations they discussed earlier. Write the nine fruits of the Spirit listed in Galatians 5:22-23 on a chalkboard or newsprint while they move. Ask: *Which fruit of the Spirit does your partner need most to face the situation s/he described to you? Why? Name the fruit you are holding and give it to your partner.* (In other words, what does it look like when a particular fruit of the Spirit guides an action toward authority figures?)

If you *did not* do **Option B** under Connect, modify the instructions above as follows: Ask participants to turn to a person next to them and give him or her a fruit of the Spirit. They should name their fruits based on what they know about the world they live in and what they know about this particular person.

Suggested benediction: *Remember who you are—you are given the Holy Spirit as a touchstone for doing the right thing.*

LOOK AHEAD

If you are planning to use the extender session after Session 6, you will need to round up some guests. Pray that the Spirit will guide you to the right people.

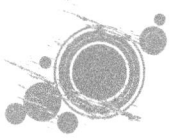

"The Lord asks everything of us, and in return he offers us true life, the happiness for which we were created. He wants us to be saints and not to settle for a bland and mediocre existence. The call to holiness is present in various ways from the very first pages of the Bible."

Pope Francis
On the Call to Holiness in Today's World, 1.

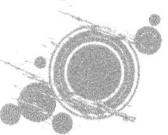

> If you can get youth to question what spirit governs their attitudes and behavior, you will have taught them something about ethics.

DISCERNING GOD'S WILL

"The place God calls you to is where your deep gladness and the world's deep hunger meet."

Frederick Buechner

"The deepest vocational question is not 'What ought I do with my life?' It is the more elemental and demanding, 'Who am I? What is my nature?'"

Parker Palmer
Let Your Life Speak

INSIGHTS FROM SCRIPTURE

Young people may associate the Holy Spirit with the highly charged emotional experience they had at camp last summer or a particularly zesty style of worship they've seen or heard. Galatians 5:13-26 points to a different kind of Spirit experience: the presence of the Holy Spirit as a touchstone for doing the right thing.

The book of Galatians is a personal letter from Paul to a church in conflict. The Galatian Christians were a mix of Jews and Gentiles wrangling over whether male Gentiles needed to be circumcised when they became Christians. Jews were circumcised on the eighth day after birth. They understood it as an act of initiation into the covenant community commanded by God ever since Abraham. Practically speaking, circumcision was a mark of identity that set Jews apart from their pagan neighbors. At times, they were persecuted for this practice and fought ferociously for the right to maintain it as a symbol of their identity. Gentiles, meanwhile, had no such history.

Although the authority these early congregations were struggling with appears to be an abstraction—the Jewish law—it was no doubt embodied by numerous aunts, uncles, parents, grandparents, and cousins who disapproved of worshiping with uncircumcised people. Paul's description of Peter not eating with Gentiles when other Jews were around (Galatians 2:11-14) is an example of how this situation played out.

At first glance, the conflict that troubled the Galatian Church seems remote. But the underlying question is still with us today: What are the marks of a Christian identity?

MARKS OF CHRISTIAN IDENTITY

Paul insisted that the mark of Christian identity it is not primarily a ritual or the keeping of a particular set of laws but rather the **presence of the Holy Spirit**. He counseled the Galatians to "keep in step with the Spirit" (vs. 25, NIV) and provided practical tips for recognizing its presence or absence.

Amazingly enough, this ancient bit of advice written by a Jew with bad health and a sharp tongue may still have something to say to North American youth, who today have far more freedom than most people from most other times and places. They may see religion as a narrow-minded collection of antiquated rules cramping their style. "So you're a Christian; what can't you do?" We desperately need Paul's insistence that the story is far bigger than that—it's about the gift of the Holy Spirit, and about Jesus, who was killed for showing the right way to live.

You may find it helpful to reflect on the following before you lead this session:

What does it mean to be free? Today we might tend to picture freedom as the opportunity to lie on a beach all day. But in the New Testament, freedom is always freedom *for* as well as freedom *from*. Being freed *from* fear and the power of death does not mean we may do whatever we please. It means we are free to serve a more worthy authority figure, to follow a Way that leads to the abundant life God intended for all.

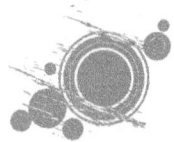

24   In Real Life | Do the Right Thing

How can I describe the Holy Spirit? Below are some passages for further study:

- Genesis 1:1-2 (The Spirit as God's creative energy)
- Ezekiel 37:1-14 (The Spirit as life-giving breath)
- Acts 2:1-13 (The coming of the Spirit at Pentecost)
- John 16:5-15 (The Holy Spirit as a counselor or advocate)
- Mark 1:9-13 (The Spirit descending at Jesus' baptism like a dove)
- 1 Cor. 12:1-13 (The Spirit as the glue unifying the body of Christ)

What does nonconformity based on the Holy Spirit look like? Many Christians have the sense that they ought to be different from the world around them, but they are not sure how. Sometimes they fall into relying on "markers" such as distinctive dress, abstaining from dancing or drinking, or eating certain foods. Whatever their original purpose, these markers often become rigid and function as laws. How is your church different from other social groups in your community? Which ways are based on old laws and which seem genuinely rooted in an active Holy Spirit?

It is not easy to discern the presence of the Holy Spirit and make it one's guiding authority. It requires the willingness to balance the courage of individual conscience with the wisdom of the faith community. It takes a willingness to question *and* listen for an answer, to be uncomfortable, even ridiculed, if the decision is out of step with an unquestioning, mob mentality.

This is probably the most difficult session of this series to lead. But if you can get participants to question what spirit governs their attitudes and behavior, you will have taught them something about ethics. Help them ask: Is this action or attitude ultimately life-affirming, or is it life-denying?

If you learn to question what spirit governs your attitudes and behavior, you will have learned something about ethics. Ask yourself: Is this action (or attitude) ultimately life-affirming, or is it life-denying?

Hot Milk Sponge Cake

In Real Life — Exploring tough questions facing youth today

Note: **Step 2** must be completed by a male, **step 3** must be completed by a female, **step 4** must be completed in total silence, **step 5** must be completed by a person with green socks (**or** no socks) while standing on one foot.

Cooking utensils needed (enough for two cakes):
- mixing bowls
- measuring spoons and cups
- saucepan
- rubber scrapers
- cake pans
- stove

1. Preheat oven to 325°F (165°C)
2. In mixing bowl, beat well: **2 eggs**
3. Add the following, then beat until light:
    - **1 cup granulated sugar**
    - **1 teaspoon vanilla**
4. Combine separately:
    - **1 cup flour**
    - **1 teaspoon baking powder**
    - **¼ teaspoon salt**

   Fold dry ingredients into egg mixture.
5. Bring to boil in a small saucepan:
    - **½ cup milk**
    - **1 teaspoon margarine**

   Add slowly to batter, stirring gently. Pour into 7x12-inch (18x30 cm) cake pan. Bake 30-35 minutes.

Do the Right Thing : Session 3

What is freedom?

Read the first phrase of Galatians 5:13 and stop after "sisters." Review in your mind what you've learned about freedom so far. Then read the rest of the passage with an eye for what Paul had in mind when he claims we are free.

Permission is granted to photocopy this handout for use with this session.

In Real Life
Exploring tough questions facing youth today

>>> SESSION 4

DEATH BY DECEIT >>>

>>> FAITH IDENTITY

We are members of a faith community that expects integrity: the body of Christ.

>>> KEY VERSES

But a man named Ananias, with the consent of his wife Sapphira, sold a piece of property; with his wife's knowledge, he kept back some of the proceeds, and brought only a part and laid it at the apostles' feet. (Acts 5:1-2)

>>> FAITH STORY

Acts 5:1-11

>>> FAITH FOCUS

Ananias and Sapphira lied to their church community about the money they gained selling a property. When they were caught, both of them fell down dead. Honesty and integrity are essential to covenant relationships; if people cease to trust one another with the truth, they soon cease to be in relationship.

>>> SESSION GOAL

Help participants to trust their faith community as a resource for struggles with right and wrong rather than resorting to dishonesty.

>>> Materials needed and advance preparation

- Newsprint/marker or chalkboard/chalk
- Index cards—several for each person
- Pens or pencils
- Rope or clothesline with signs that say "Totally unacceptable" and "Sort of okay." Stretch the line across one wall of the room and put one of the signs at each end.
- Clothespins
- Bibles
- Couple to play Ananias and Sapphira (*Option B* in Explore)
- White writing paper (*Option D* in Apply)

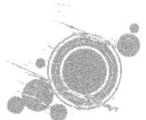

TEACHING PLAN

1. FOCUS 5-10 minutes

>>> **Option A:** Have the group divide into pairs and tell each other something about their week, with this additional instruction: **What they say may be true or it may be a believable lie.** Then discuss the experience as a group. *What is it like to lie to someone you know? What is it like to listen to someone and not know whether or not they are telling the truth? Did you find this exercise hard or easy?*

>>> **Option B:** Write this question on the board: **What would a society look like where no one could be trusted to tell the truth?** Have the group break into pairs and come up with mini-skits that illustrate this kind of a nightmare world. For example, one pair might play a scene between a store clerk and a shopper who is informed that the price on the item he wants to buy is not really true. If your group is small, you can all work together.

In Real Life | Do the Right Thing 27

»»» WHAT PAYOFF IN HONESTY?

Some corporations send insincere messages when they require employees to report wrongdoing, and then destroy the careers of those who blow the whistle. Whistleblowers will tell you that while they are treated like criminals for exposing wrongdoing, those who do wrong often remain in their jobs unpunished and unrepentant. Whistleblowers "can't be trusted," and those who promote the company at any cost are rewarded. Corporations want people who are honest, but not too honest.

» **Option C:** Challenge your group with the following brain teaser called **The Liar and the Truth-Teller:**

While walking down a country road on your way to a town you've never been to before, you come to a fork in the road, and you don't know which road to take. Two men are sitting beside the road, so you ask them, "Which way to town?" They point to a sign behind them that says: "For $5 these men each answer any question that can be answered yes or no. One always tells the truth, the other always lies. Good luck." How can you get reliable directions to town without spending more than $5?

Give participants up to 4 minutes to come up with the answer. If they don't, suggest that one answer that would do the job is, "If I asked your brother if this road (point to one fork) will take me to town, what would he say?" A "no" answer means the road *will* take you to town; a "yes" answer means it will not, since no matter who you asked, you would be getting the opposite of the truth. There may be other possible correct answers.

Whether or not they come up with the answer on their own, briefly follow up by asking: *What if you had to live in a world where you could never quite tell who was telling the truth and who was lying?*

2. CONNECT 10 minutes

Pass around a pack of index cards and have each person take several. Ask each one to think of at least three situations in which it is tempting to be dishonest and write each one on a card. They could be lies participants have witnessed, seen in the media, or even told themselves.

Then pass out clothespins and ask each person to clip their cards to the rope you have strung across the room. Point out that one end of the rope says, "Totally unacceptable" and the other end says, "Sort of okay." Ask participants to decide where along this line their lies belong. Give them some time to mill around the clothesline and see what other people came up with.

Shift to the next activity: While participants are doing this, write a card of your own that says, "You tell your church you are going to sell some property and give this money for a special need. When the property sells, you only give a part of the money to the church but pretend it is the whole amount." Ask your group where on the line they think you should put this card. Then say, *Did you know this situation actually happened in the early church? Two people died because of this lie.*

3. EXPLORE THE BIBLE 8-12 minutes.

» **Option A:** Pass around Bibles and have participants turn to Acts 5:1-11. Ask a good reader to read the story aloud. Ananias and Sapphira's untimely end will be new to many of your participants. Their story is not a popular one. The harsh judgment that falls on this mixed-up couple and the expectations that the early church placed on its members with regard to wealth make it tempting to avoid this story. But its prickly edges and unexpected consequences make it a good discussion starter:

- *How do you feel about what happened to Ananias and Sapphira?*
- *Why do you think this unpleasant story is included in the Bible?* (See some suggestions in Insights from Scripture.)

Refresh memories of what was happening to help participants see where the story of Ananias and Sapphira fits in the book of Acts. Stress how this faith community was formed and what kinds of things were taking place there. (Skim through the first few chapters of Acts and/or see Insights from Scripture.)

>> **Option B:** The story of Ananias and Sapphira also provides plenty of drama for a role-play. If you have time to set up this scenario, it may be an especially effective way to tell the story.

Find a respected couple in your congregation willing to play Ananias and Sapphira. Tell your participants that this couple has decided to sell _____ (a car, a boat, a computer, etc.—something everyone knows they own) and donate the money to a service project your participants are involved with or aware of. When Ananias comes in to present the check, you play Peter and question him about the amount. You, like the early church, will then have to decide what to do with two dead bodies. You could have a few burly youth carry them out or you could leave them lying on the floor for the rest of the meeting. If Ananias and Sapphira aren't willing to play dead that long, they can revive and join your group for the rest of the discussion.

You might also consider a "take 2" where Ananias and Sapphira come to your room and explain their dilemma to the group. "We would like to give this money to the church as we promised," they might say, "but now we would also like to keep a part of it to buy _____ for ourselves." Would it be okay if they just give part of the money? Let the group discuss and decide.

4. APPLY 13-15 minutes

>> **Option A:** Here are some questions to consider together:

- *How is lying to people you are close to especially destructive?*
- *Is lying and cheating still wrong when the other party is not an individual? What about lying to a company or the government?*
- *What about cheating a person you don't respect? Is this still lying to God, as Peter says in 5:4?*
- *Many churches have a sharing time during worship when members can share personal concerns. Often, people bring up world situations or relatives with health problems. Have you ever heard anybody bring an ethical problem before the group for prayer? How do you think your congregation would respond? Do you think your church is a place where people can be real about what's bothering them?*
- *If you were having some struggles with right and wrong, would you go to your church (or youth group) for help? Why or why not?*
- *Do churches deserve to be trusted? What if people have good reason not to trust their faith community with their struggles?*

>> **Option B:** Return to your clothesline of lies and talk about the situations described. In each case ask, *What relationship is violated by this lie?* Try to find faces for lies that seem to have no victim. For example, cheating on income tax might harm a poor person who depends on government-funded aid programs. Remind participants that whether they consider themselves members of the body of Christ or not, they are all members of the larger human community. This community will also disintegrate if no one can be trusted to tell the truth. Would anybody like to move a lie from one position on the line to another?

>> **Option C:** Ask for volunteers to share specific situations they have wrestled with that involved honesty. This might be a lie they've told or some other ethical issue they've struggled with but kept hidden. How can the group help? One way to help start a discussion like this is to share from your own life and struggles. Remind your group that this is not a gossip session. If a person asks for confidentiality, what is shared must stay in the group.

>>> **Option D:** Pass out paper and drawing materials and ask your participants to draw a picture of a lie they have told or a corner of their lives they are not ready to be honest about. The picture need not be literal or recognizable. Then encourage them to think of a way they might begin to share this lie or problem area with someone. Have them write down a "step 1" on the back of the paper.

5. RESPOND 8 minutes

Your discussion above can lead to your bringing up the idea of a "Decision Clinic" or "Clearness Committee," as suggested in the introduction to this unit. Would your youth welcome a place where they could come with tough questions about right and wrong? If not, don't push it; if so, get them to help you implement this idea.

Have everyone gather in a circle for a prayer. If you used **Option B** or **Option D** in Apply, place the index cards with lies or the pictures in the center of the circle. Allow time for silence in the prayer, as well as for sentence prayers of encouragement and support in struggles with specific situations of integrity that were raised.

Note: If you are planning to invite a panel of adults for the extender session, now is a good time to seek youth input on who they might like to hear from and what questions they might like to hear addressed.

Suggested benediction: *Remember who you are—you are part of a community that expects integrity: the body of Christ.*

>>> LOOK AHEAD

For next session, round up a woman willing to be accused of adultery. Some options in the activities also ask for a variety of props and news articles.

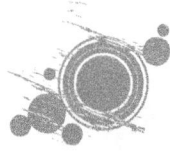

 # INSIGHTS FROM SCRIPTURE

TRUTH ABOUT LYING

The book of Acts describes the formation of the early church. Its first few chapters are especially dramatic ones: The Holy Spirit swoops down on gathered believers at Pentecost, fisherman Peter preaches stirring sermons that astonish the highly educated, disciples are arrested and a crippled beggar is healed. Acts 2:42-47 tells us that the believers had everything in common, meeting together and eating together daily. Acts 4:32 tells us they were one in heart and mind.

HARSH, DUDE!

It is interesting, though, that Luke does not use the word "ekklesia" (church) to describe this new community until they had been through a test. The story of Ananias and Sapphira is a shocking one. Two people were left dead in the wake of a lie and a whole community of believers trembled with fear. One commentator calls it "almost unchristian."

How could such a harsh and unforgiving account have worked its way into the Bible? Probably because it is true in at least two ways. First of all, what happened to Ananias and Sapphira makes sense given what we know about the human body. Doctors and psychologists tell us that living with secrets puts enormous stress on the human body. People who live with lies are often physically unhealthy as well. It is not hard to imagine this kind of stress leading to a heart attack or stroke. The suddenness of this couple's death when confronted dramatically underlines the emotional and physical effects of living a lie.

Secondly, what happened to Ananias and Sapphira highlights what we know about the body of Christ. Honesty and integrity are essential to covenant relationships; if people cease to trust each other with the truth, they soon cease to be in relationship. Money was not the only thing Ananias and Sapphira held back from the body of Christ—they also held back their struggle with money.

Their story might have been different if they had had the courage to be honest with the apostles and say, "We're not sure we are ready to part with this." Most people who leave the church are not carried out on a stretcher; they just wander away. But more often than not, they leave because they feel they must hide a part of themselves from their faith community. The bitter truth is that we cannot be part of the body of Christ and live a lie. If we try it, our relationship with that community will soon die.

The book of Acts is careful not to draw too many theological conclusions from this incident involving a lie. It does not say that Ananias and Sapphira's death was the judgment of God. Nor does it claim that this is what is in store for all liars. It merely tells us what happened to two particular people at a particular time in the church's history and suggests we have something to learn from them.

For all its resilience through the centuries, the body of Christ is a fragile thing. It cannot exist if members do not trust each other. If Christ is the cornerstone of this enterprise, integrity is the cement that holds the stones in place around it.

A group who used this session discussed lies such as cheating on a test, lying to parents about where you were going, and lying to a person you did not want to date. Lying about where you were going was wrong and dangerous, they reasoned, because you could get hurt and no one would know where you were. But most group members were not bothered by occasional cheating on schoolwork or evading an unwanted date.

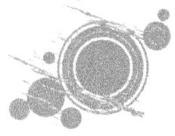

SESSION 5

THE FIRST STONE

FAITH IDENTITY

We believe in a God who leaves the door open for change.

KEY VERSE

And Jesus said, "Neither do I condemn you. Go your way, and from now on do not sin again." (John 8:11)

FAITH STORY

John 8:2-11

FAITH FOCUS

The Pharisees brought a woman caught in adultery to Jesus in order to test his loyalty to the law. Jesus said that anyone who was without sin could stone her. When her accusers left, Jesus set the woman free and told her not to sin again. But the story of the woman taken in adultery is not really a story about women or adultery; it is a story about Pharisees being pushed to think about their own sins instead of just pointing out other people's.

SESSION GOAL

Encourage participants to turn sin into a new start through Christ's forgiveness and the faith community's support.

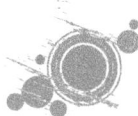

TEACHING PLAN

1. FOCUS 6 minutes

Option A: Start with sin. In our culture, the word "sin" has a narrow and shallow meaning. It is often used sarcastically and applied mainly to sexual misbehavior. Most people find the word judgmental and avoid it. The biblical understanding of sin is much richer.

Here are some ways the Bible talks about sin and suggestions for representing them with concrete objects:

- sin as an incurable wound (bandages and medicine)
- sin as being enslaved (handcuffs or a chain)
- sin as brokenness (a torn family photo)
- sin as uncleanness (a medical toxic waste sign or stained cloth)
- sin as missing the mark (an arrow and target)

Materials needed and advance preparation

- Props for *Option A* in Focus
- Stack of newspapers and magazines (*Option B* in Focus)
- Paper and pencils or pens
- Beanbags, paper wads, aging vegetables or other things to throw, one per person (see Explore the Bible)
- Stick-on nametags (one per person). Come up with a list of sins and write a sin on each nametag.
- Someone willing to play the woman caught in adultery. Have her wear a large cardboard placard with a red "A" on it, and ask her to wait outside the room until you give the signal to enter.
- News articles for *Option B* in Apply
- Copies of the handout sheet for Session 5 (*Option A* in Respond)
- Chalkboard/chalk or newsprint/marker
- Media player for video (*Option B* in Respond)
- Song books (*Option C* in Respond)

Assemble a collection of these objects (or simple drawings of them) and have them laid out on a table as people enter. Ask your group to figure out what the things on the table have in common. Let them guess for a bit and then tell them, *These things all represent biblical ways of talking about what it feels like to have sinned.* Briefly go over the list above.

Go to Connect, **Option A**.

>> **Option B:** Start with forgiveness. Pass around a stack of newspapers or magazines and ask participants to find examples of ways our society handles wrongdoing—references to prisons, lawsuits, fines, the death penalty, etc. Also have them mark any occurrences they can find of the words "confession" and "forgiveness."

Go to Connect, **Option B**.

2. CONNECT 3-4 minutes

>> **Option A:** Ask participants how *they* would describe what it feels like to have done something wrong. What objects or word pictures might help? This will be easiest if you encourage them to think of specific instances when they did the wrong thing. Paper and pencil for doodling might help. Do any of the biblical images make sense to them? Which seem most real?

>> **Option B:** Analyze your Focus findings and connect with youth experience:

Where in our culture do we talk about forgiveness? What kind of meaning does this word have in this day and age? Have you ever been forgiven for something?

3. EXPLORE THE BIBLE 6-7 minutes

Shift to this activity by saying: *The Bible passage we're going to look at is one that some people love and some people hate. It's about someone who sinned and got away with it—sort of. Let's see what **you** think.*

Tell everyone they will get to participate in this story, but first they need two things. Pass around the beanbags or paper wads that you brought and see that everyone has one. Next, take out the "sin" nametags you prepared and stick one on each person's forehead without showing the bearer what the tag says. Tell them not to let their friends know what is written on their foreheads just yet. The sins you use need not necessarily be "youth" sins.

Some examples of sins you might use:

- I told racist jokes.
- I divorced my wife so I could marry a younger woman.
- I polluted the environment.
- I cheated on my taxes.
- I was disrespectful to my parents.
- I wasted my life on screen time.

While participants are getting their items to throw and examining one another's foreheads, check to see that your "woman caught in adultery" is ready to make an entrance. Begin reading John 8:2-11 aloud. The woman enters during verse 3 wearing the large letter "A" as in *The Scarlet Letter*. Be sure you look at your participants when you read "*Now what do you say?*" in verse 5. Stop after verse 8.

>> **YOUTH EXPLAIN, "WHEN PEOPLE DO THE WRONG THING...**

- they usually get suspended or expelled."
- it spreads all around the school."
- maybe their friends miss them, but most kids don't care."
- teachers are glad they're gone."

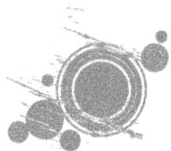

Tell participants they get to be the Pharisees today. They are free to pelt the actress with paper wads if the sticker on their foreheads is blank. In order to find this out, they will need to ask each other what their tags say by asking yes-or-no questions.

Allow a minute or two for everyone to find out what they are wearing on their foreheads and then finish the passage. The woman taken in adultery may then leave or join the discussion.

4. APPLY 10 minutes

>> **Option A:** Collect nametags and paper wads and settle your group back into their seats. This passage offers many interesting points for discussion. Choose from the questions below.

- *Was Jesus too easy on the woman caught in adultery? How do you feel about his response? What if she were a child abuser?*
- *Do you think we need punishments to keep people from doing the wrong thing? How does knowing that forgiveness is possible affect people's decision making?*
- *What does it feel like to be forgiven? Have you ever experienced this?*
- *Why do we often focus on sexual sin when we use the word "sin"? What other kinds of behavior are sins but are often not given that label?*
- *If you were caught in a sin (stealing, cheating, gluttony, abusing someone or something), how would you want your church to respond to you?*
- *How do you know what is a sin and what isn't? What if you and your church don't agree?*

>> **Option B:** Jesus was called upon to judge the adulterous woman because the Pharisees were trying to trap him. Find issues in your local news or church bulletins in which public discussion of right and wrong has turned toward scoring points against one's enemies rather than helping the people caught in the problem. Abortion, homosexuality, and clericalism are issues where heated conflicts or power struggles often happen. Bring in and discuss articles that illustrate examples of this behavior or creative alternatives to it.

5. RESPOND 20 minutes

>> **Option A:** Distribute copies of the handout sheet and choose one of the two case studies to work on. If your group is larger than 10, split into several discussion groups. If you feel that one or both of the cases is not appropriate for your group, write your own case study. Perhaps there is a live issue in your congregation you could work on.

Ask the group(s) to come up with a **plan** (as opposed to vague good intentions) that could help the characters mentioned work through sin and forgiveness in healthy ways. The plan should have at least three steps and be written down so that participants are encouraged to work at this with some discipline and precision.

Draw attention to "Questions to Consider" on the handout sheet. These can guide their planning. When everyone is finished, share the plans and write them on the newsprint or chalkboard.

>> **Option B:** View a video featuring a talk (http://www.ted.com/talks/brene_brown_on_vulnerability) by vulnerability researcher Brené Brown. She studies human connection—our ability to empathize, belong, and love. In a poignant, funny talk, she shares a deep insight from her research. Follow the video with brief discussion with the group, closing with a prayer that your faith community can be a place where sins can be dealt with safely and where people can be forgiven.

>>> **Option C:** Distribute song books. Have your group find examples of songs or readings relating to confession and forgiveness. Responses could include singing a song, having participants write confessions of their own, or selecting a worship resource to go with one of the case studies.

Close with a prayer for your faith community, that it may be a place where sins can be dealt with safely and where people can be forgiven.

Suggested benediction: *Remember who you are—you are known by a God who leaves the door open for change.*

>>>
LOOK AHEAD

Read over the extender session if you plan to use it after Session 6. Find 3-4 adults willing to participate in a panel discussion. Include a range of ages as well as a priest, deacon, or religious sister or brother so that you have someone with enough breadth of experience to talk about how the faith community at large works through difficult ethical issues.

INSIGHTS FROM SCRIPTURE

No unit on doing the *right* thing would be complete without a session on what to do when someone has done the *wrong* thing. It's easy to make good choices when everyone has always done so, and no past history of mistakes needs to be untangled. But rarely are we so lucky. Being the people of God means learning to pick up the pieces and offer new life even when wrong has been done.

The story of the woman taken in adultery is not really a story about women or adultery; it is a story about Pharisees. No doubt this is why this text makes people uncomfortable. It is included in a section of John where Jesus is in bitter conflict with Jewish leaders. The Pharisees were challenging his authority and the temple police had made several attempts to arrest him.

›› CATCH-22

The incident with the guilty woman was another attempt to trap Jesus. Although the law of Moses did permit stoning in clear-cut cases of adultery, many people considered this punishment too harsh and it was rarely practiced. Roman law did not permit the Jews to execute people without Roman permission and Rome did not execute adulterers. This put Jesus in a catch-22. If he said the woman should be stoned, he was in trouble with Roman law and would alienate many of the people who were listening; if he said she should not be stoned, he was in trouble with Jewish law and would appear soft on sin. Meanwhile a woman stood alone, humiliated and condemned, the pawn of warring religious factions.

Jesus opted for a third way. He turned this test into a challenge for the Pharisees by pushing them to think about their own sins instead of just point out other people's. Then he set the woman free and encouraged her to start over.

›› TOUGH-LOVE FORGIVENESS

The story of the woman caught in adultery is incomplete by itself. It does not tell us if the woman repented and changed her lifestyle. It does not show a faith community at work in the process. It does not even mention forgiveness. But this brief moment points us toward a key of Jesus' ministry. The chance to "go and sin no more" lies at the very heart of the good news Christians proclaim and is at the very heart of God. Tough-love forgiveness remains a constant from Noah's rainbow to Moses' glimpse of God's back on Mount Sinai to the parable of the "foolish father" and his undeserving son (the Prodigal Son).

For better or for worse, God insists on sharing this stressful job of forgiveness with us. Jesus charged his disciples with the authority to forgive sins (see John 20:22-23, for example). Part of what it means to be a faith community is to be a place where sin can be addressed without crushing the sinner or minimizing the suffering the sin may have brought to others. Like Jesus with the woman caught in adultery, we are called to stand between sinners and those they have wronged and work toward healing.

Faith communities ought to be expert in dealing with sin and forgiveness. Often, they are not. Your youth may have some sarcastic things to say about how well the church has lived up to its calling. And they may be right. But in a world of lawsuits and liability, saving face and seeking revenge, they need the vision of another way.

The 1st STONE

In Real Life
Exploring tough questions facing youth today

Case Study #1

Michelle is not involved with any church, but has attended several youth functions with her boyfriend Timothy who is part of the group. Her best female friend, Emma, is also in this youth group. One day Michelle tells Emma that she's pregnant. She has told Timothy but is afraid to tell his parents. She wants Emma to come with her to get an abortion. How could Emma, Timothy, and their youth group respond to this situation in ways that might confront wrongdoing but also offer new life and a new beginning to both Michelle and Timothy?

Case Study #2

Trevor and Jake used to be close friends. They are part of the same youth group. Lately they've drifted apart and found different friends. One night at a party, Trevor talks with a girl who says her boyfriend shoplifted the expensive leather jacket she is wearing. She says he's part of a group that does it on dares. They started stealing packs of cards and candy bars and worked up from there. She also mentions drug use. Trevor knows Jake is part of this group. Trevor is bothered by the idea that Jake is probably shoplifting and possibly getting into drugs. When he confronts Jake about it alone, Jake says it's none of his business but doesn't deny the shoplifting. Trevor is worried because he still cares about Jake. What could Trevor try next? Or should he just give up?

QUESTIONS TO CONSIDER

- What brokenness or wrongdoing needs to be named before healing can take place?
- Who needs to be involved? Is it something youth can handle themselves? If not, what adults might be helpful?
- What are some examples of behavior that would *not* be helpful?
- What if the parties involved don't think they've done anything wrong? Are there times when forgiveness and a new beginning are *not* possible?

Permission is granted to photocopy this handout for use with this session.

>>> SESSION 6

THE NEEDLE'S EYE >>>

>>> FAITH IDENTITY

We are representatives of a God who cares about the poor.

>>> KEY VERSE

[Jesus said,] "It is easier for a camel to go through the eye of a needle than for someone who is rich to enter the kingdom of God." (Mark 10:25)

>>> FAITH STORY

Mark 10:17-31

>>> FAITH FOCUS

A man ran up to Jesus and asked what he must do to inherit eternal life. When Jesus heard that this man had already kept all of the commandments, he told him to sell what he had and give it to the poor. The man went away sad because he was wealthy. Jesus' disciples were left puzzling over this hard teaching.

>>> SESSION GOAL

Confront participants with Jesus' persistent attention to wealth and poverty and invite them to begin asking questions about the ethics of economic injustice.

>>> Materials needed and advance preparation

- Chalkboard/chalk or newsprint/marker
- Tokens (play money, pennies, dry beans), enough for about 5 per person (*Option A in Focus*)
- Doughnuts or another snack (*Option A in Focus*)
- Stack of storebought clothing with manufacturer's labels (*only necessary* if your group is smaller than six); also, brief research of average annual income in the countries where they were made (*Option B in Focus*)
- Threaded needles, enough for everyone; also one length of yarn or string too thick to thread through a needle
- Bibles
- Copies of the handout sheet for Session 6

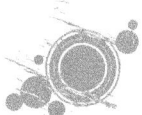 # TEACHING PLAN

1. FOCUS 10 minutes

>>> **Option A:** Begin with a game that illustrates how wealth becomes unequally distributed. Write the following rules on a chalkboard or newsprint. Distribute tokens, giving some people three tokens, some four, and some five.

Rules:

1. Object: Earn enough tokens to buy a doughnut. Doughnuts cost 10 tokens.
2. Earn tokens by challenging other players one at a time and asking to see their hands. The person with more tokens gets to take a token from the "poorer" person. If both players have the same number of tokens, nothing happens.
3. Do not let anybody know how much "money" you have unless challenged. If challenged, you *must* show your hands.
4. You cannot challenge the same person twice in a row.

In Real Life | Do the Right Thing 39

Display several doughnuts and point out how appetizing they are, but don't let the group see how many you brought. Scarcity drives the economy! Play the game until at least one or two people can buy a doughnut.

Note: If you have a very small group, add "ghost" players.

>> **Option B:** *(for both Focus and Connect):* Skip the game and begin by asking participants who they think the poor are. What do they look like? Do they have jobs or are they lazy? What contact does your group have with people financially less well off than they are? Ask them to describe the poorest person they know.

Then have each one turn to the person beside them and check the labels in the clothing they are wearing to find out where they were made. **Note:** If your group is smaller than six, bring out a stack of clothes (bought, not homemade) and have them check those labels as well.

Make a list of the countries you encounter. Ask participants if they have any idea what the average per capita *yearly* income of people in these countries is. (Invite someone in the group to quickly research this via an Internet connection; or bring out your own list of approximate incomes.) Point out that we are regularly fed and clothed by people we don't know who may or may not be paid a living wage. Very few of them enjoy the lifestyle we take for granted.

>> **Option C:** *(for both Focus and Connect):* Ask participants to describe the richest person they know and the poorest person they know.

2. CONNECT 7 minutes

(Use this activity only if you played the game with tokens in Focus.)

Collect the tokens and bring the group back together to process what happened.

- *How did those who started with only three tokens fare?*
- *What did the people who ended up with doughnuts do differently from everyone else?*
- *How do those who were left hungry feel about those who got a doughnut?*
- *What strategies worked or didn't work in this game?*
- *Which rule annoyed you most?*

Move from the game experience to real-life experience. What stereotypes does your group have about rich people and poor people? List the top 10 stereotypes. Did this game change anybody's perceptions about why some people are rich and others are poor?

3. EXPLORE THE BIBLE 10 minutes

Shift to this activity: Hold up a needle and a piece of yarn or thread too thick to go through the needle's eye. Invite someone to try to thread the needle. Then say, *Most of us think that poverty is a problem and wealth is not a problem. Jesus saw things differently. Let's see what he had to say about wealth and what it has to do with the eye of a needle.*

Have everyone turn to Mark 10:17-31 and read the story of the rich young man together. The story is mainly dialog so you can use a number of voices. Assign the following parts: narrator, Jesus, rich person, Peter/disciples. After you have all heard the story, ask participants to reread it on their own and come up with an answer to these questions: *Why isn't it enough to keep the commandments? Why does doing the right thing require thinking about possessions? Where and how does this challenge you personally?* Share from the Insights from Scripture on God's passionate concern for the disadvantaged and the Christian's role as representatives of that concern.

4. APPLY 10 minutes

>> **Option A:** (*Use if you used Option A in Focus*) Distribute another round of three, four, and five tokens to each person. Take about a quarter of the group aside and tell them privately to play the game differently this time. They are to try to see that everyone receives a doughnut. Give them time to huddle and come up with a plan. They may ignore the rules of the game as necessary.

As they huddle, take the rest of the participants aside and instruct them to play the game as they did at the beginning of the meeting and to see that no one breaks any of the original rules. Play until everyone has a doughnut or until everyone is thoroughly frustrated. Then discuss what happened:

- *What was it like to try to do something different with your tokens? Did it work?*
- *How long did it take for the group playing by the original rules to figure out what was going on? What conflicts resulted?*

Point out that Jesus' words on wealth in this passage include both a hard teaching and grace ("for God all things are possible," vs. 27). We have not really grappled with the reign of God until we have grappled with the power our possessions have over us. But neither are we able to earn our way into God's presence simply by keeping all the religious laws. We have not understood this passage until we have heard both those messages.

>> **Option B:** Exhausted with trying to keep up with the pressures of consuming? Try getting rid of things you don't use. Pair participants who will promise to help each other go through closets and garages to find every item they haven't used in a year and donate it to an organization or recycle it. Then, don't buy anything for a month. If you see something you want, put it on a list to wait until the month is up. You are likely to find that you don't really want the things on the list by the time you get around to buying them.

5. RESPOND 8 minutes

End this unit with a symbolic gift and a guided blessing. Ask participants to close their eyes and settle into silence. Then read the following, pausing between each paragraph.

Remember who you are—
you are heirs to the story of a loving Creator worth worshiping.
Remember who you are—
you are followers of a Christ who died rather than harm others.
Remember who you are—
you are given the Holy Spirit as a touchstone for doing the right thing.
Remember who you are—
you are part of a community that expects integrity: the body of Christ.
Remember who you are—
you are known by a God who leaves the door open for change.
Remember who you are—
you represent a God who cares about the poor.
Remember who you are—you are a camel.
Your knees are knobby... you are not too bright...
you have a homely face and a stubborn temperament...
you have fleas.
You are carrying a huge pack on your back, stuffed with things.
And now imagine a wind, stronger than any wind you've ever experienced.
The wind is sucking you toward a tiny opening. You want to go with the wind but you are afraid. What is on the other side of that opening? The wind is pulling and pulling .... Your face feels like it is caught in a vice. You can't breathe.... The needle's eye is hard, sharp, unyielding .... It compresses your whole body and scrapes the pack off your back. What was in that pack?
Now your hump is stuck. You cannot move a muscle. You want to give up and die. But the wind will not give up. It is still pulling; squeezing you into a new shape.... Hours go by.... Then suddenly, you hear a loud pop and it's over. With God, all things are possible. Welcome to the reign of God.

Now choose one or both of the following closings:

- The handout sheet for this session is a poster with the "Remember Who You Are" sayings on it. Give each person a copy with a threaded needle stuck in the upper right-hand corner.
- If your group is Twitter or Facebook savvy, set prompts to send each participant one of the six "Remember Who You Are" reminders each month.

INSIGHTS FROM SCRIPTURE

Although the Bible is silent on many perplexing ethical issues that trouble us today, wealth and poverty is not one of them. Biblical writers from Amos to James, from Job to Luke, devoted more attention to economics than any other ethical issue. In fact, there are many, many more verses in the Bible about poverty and wealth than there are about sexuality. What drives this concern is not that wealth is bad; in the ancient scriptures it is seen as a blessing. But God's passionate care for the poor requires the wealthy to use their position to benefit all.

Passages such as Deuteronomy 10:17-19 are typical throughout the Hebrew Bible: "For the Lord your God is God of gods and Lord of lords, the great God, mighty and awesome, who is not partial and takes no bribe, who executes justice for the orphan and the widow, and who loves the strangers, providing them food and clothing. You shall also love the stranger, for you were strangers in the land of Egypt." The demand for justice for the poor is grounded in the Israelites' own experience as slaves and the underlying assumption that to be human means to be made in the image of God. We are God's flesh and blood representatives in the world, and God gets mighty annoyed at being misrepresented.

In Mark 10:17-31, a man treated Jesus with almost exaggerated reverence but then was unable to follow him because of what it meant for him monetarily. No doubt this was one of the stories early Christians told and retold when they were wrestling with economic inequalities in their midst. Perhaps it became part of the Bible because it speaks to a particularly thorny problem: What do we do with people who call Jesus Lord but are not willing to put their possessions under his lordship?

> For the bored, the restless, and the desperate, there is only one option: GO. Grapple with wealth, grapple with poverty; sell what you have and follow to a place where you begin again to hunger for the reign of God.

NO SIMPLE ANSWERS

The story of the rich young man is a good one for participants because there are no simple answers and no simple villains—not even the young man who walks away sad. Mark 10:17-31 maintains a tension between Jesus' hard teaching on possessions and his words of grace. Note that 10:21 says that Jesus loved the rich young man who questioned him. This is the only place in the Gospel of Mark that describes Jesus as loving a particular person. And while the young man went away sad and the disciples were distressed, Jesus came out of the encounter with a sense of humor. God can do the impossible, his comment on camels insists, even save rich people!

PERSONAL MORALITY IS NOT ENOUGH

Youth may also resonate with the restlessness the young man in this story felt. Here is someone who claimed he had already accomplished all that his faith required of him. He did not kill, lie, mouth off to his parents, or fool around, and he still felt empty and bored; bored enough to be seeking something with great urgency. Some of your participants may be in this boat as well. They are the ones who most need to hear the hard teaching in this text: Personal morality is not enough. It will not sustain spiritual growth for a lifetime. Nor does it satisfy Jesus' command to love God and neighbor. If the gospel leaves your participants cold, it may mean they need to leave their comfortable lives and go to a place where they can learn about hunger, need, poverty, and injustice. From this vantage point, the reign of God is much more visible and much more real.

Different members of your group many need one or the other of the twin messages in this passage: the call to lay our possessions at Jesus' feet or the assurance that God can pull reluctant camels loaded with baggage through a needle's eye.

Remember Who You Are

In Real Life — Exploring tough questions facing youth today

Remember who you are—you are followers of a Christ who died rather than harm others.

Remember who you are—you are given the Holy Spirit as a touchstone for doing the right thing.

Remember who you are—you are part of a community that expects integrity: the body of Christ.

Remember who you are—you are known by a God who leaves the door open for change.

Remember who you are—you represent a God who cares about the poor.

Remember who you are—you are heirs to the story of a loving Creator worth worshiping.

Do the Right Thing : Session 6

Permission is granted to photocopy this handout for use with this session.

>>> EXTENDER SESSION
(best used after Session 6)

SHARING WISDOM ABOUT ETHICS

>> SESSION GOAL
Connect youth with adults who can model Christ-like approaches to dilemmas of right and wrong.

>> SESSION PLAN
Faith is more likely to be caught than taught. Arrange for a panel of 3-5 adults to join your group for a session. For best results, prepare panelists in advance with the three questions below and an outline of what you've covered in this unit. Ask them to come with specific stories if possible. Pictures or show-and-tell items would also be helpful. Allow youth to help select participants and encourage them to think of interview questions in advance.

- *What ethical issues did you struggle with when you were younger?*
- *What ethical issues do you struggle with now? How are you working at them?*
- *What issues have you watched the church (current parish or the church at large) work through? What have you learned about right and wrong from this process?*

Work through the questions one at a time, giving each panelist time to contribute and youth the opportunity to ask questions.

Exploring tough questions facing youth today

CLUELESS AND CALLED
Discipleship and the Gospel of Mark

What does it take to be a disciple? This study of the Gospel of Mark focuses on the requirements for following Jesus' way and the abundant life that is ours as a result. (5 sessions)

DO MIRACLES HAPPEN?
Signs and Wonders in the Gospel of John

The greatest miracle, recorded in John 1:14 and 3:16, is the miracle of God's love that became flesh and lived among us. But John also included examples of what we more traditionally think of as miracles: the wonder of abundance from little; healing; signs of impossibility and faith; and the resurrection. (5 sessions)

DO THE RIGHT THING
Ethics Shaped by Faith

How do you know what's right and what's wrong? Even when you figure it out, the right thing is often the unpopular or unpleasant choice. This unit offers participants a clearer sense of what it means to claim a faith identity, a foundation that can help them sort out the gritty details of ethics shaped by faith. (6 sessions)

FIGHT RIGHT
A Christian Approach to Conflict Resolution

This unit will help youth understand conflict and its function. They will learn how they can be honest and loving, and explore how conflict can be used for positive results. They will also learn ways to enhance their communication skills. 1 Corinthians. (5 sessions)

GOD IS A WARRIOR?
Violence in the Bible

The Bible challenges us to be reconciled to one another and work for justice. So what do we do with the stories that seem to condone violence or even encourage it? A discussion of issues in the Old and New Testaments. (6 sessions)

HOW DO YOU KNOW?
Wisdom in the Bible

Wisdom literature teaches us that we gain knowledge of the world, ourselves, and God through experience and observation. This unit provides practical, hands-on wisdom to help young people avoid life's snares and grow closer to God. Proverbs, Job, Ecclesiastes. (5 sessions)

HOW TO BE A TRUE FRIEND
The Bible Reveals Friendship's Heart

To be a friend takes skill. Help youth discover the secrets of friendship through various stories from the Old and New Testament. (6 sessions)

HOW TO READ THE BIBLE
Building Skills for Bible Study

What kind of book is the Bible? What does this book mean to me? This unit looks at the Bible as revelation, as history, as literature. Selected scripture. (5 sessions)

KEEPING THE GARDEN
A Faith Response to God's Creation

If Christians believe that God made the world, we do not need any more compelling reason to care for it than that God has handed us a treasure to hold and protect. This unit gets beyond trendy environmentalism and challenges youth to see environmental awareness as a religious issue. Genesis. (6 sessions)

MANTRAS, MENORAHS, AND MINARETS
Encountering Other Faiths

How is Christianity different from other faiths? Why do others believe the way they do? This study can give youth a new appreciation for the uniqueness of Jesus. Selected scripture. (5 sessions)

SALT, LIGHT, AND THE GOOD LIFE
The Beatitudes and the Sermon on the Mount

What can youth expect in a life of discipleship? This unit explores the Sermon on the Mount under four main sections: the Beatitudes, Salt and Light, Jesus and the Law, and Heavenly Teachings. Matthew 5. (6 sessions)

A SPECK IN THE UNIVERSE
The Bible on Self-Esteem and Peer Pressure

Discover God's unconditional love and acceptance of all people. This study will show positive ways to have one's life make a difference, and help youth find ways to resist negative peer pressure and turn it into positive action. (6 sessions)

THE RADICAL REIGN
Parables of Jesus

Jesus used parables to reveal what the kingdom of God is like, and how God relates to us. This study highlights how the parables reveal God's reign as radically different from the world we live in, and what that means for the Christian life. (6 sessions)

TESTING THE WATERS
Basic Tenets of Faith

Discover the biblical roots for the central Christian concepts of covenant, community, and baptism. This short course is a way to test the (baptismal) waters of Christianity before diving in, or review the basics for those who already have. (6 sessions)

WHO IS GOD?
Engaging the Mystery

God is beyond human comprehension, yet desires to be known. These sessions focus on the way we get clues about and glimpses of God from the Bible, God's creation, and church tradition. Selected scripture. (5 sessions)

www.ingramcontent.com/pod-product-compliance
Lightning Source LLC
Chambersburg PA
CBHW081328190426

43193CB00043B/2855